Original title:
The Art of Inspiration

Editor: Jessica Elisabeth Luik
Author: Mariana Virelai
ISBN HARDBACK: 978-9916-86-238-4
ISBN PAPERBACK: 978-9916-86-239-1

Cradle of Imagination

Within the cradle dreams do sail,
On currents of a whispered tale.
Stars ignite with thoughts so bright,
In endless dance of day and night.

Ideas crafted, fleeting grace,
Taking form in boundless space.
From shadows deep, to light they rise,
In the cradle, wonders lie.

An infant spark, a flicker small,
Can birth a world, transcend it all.
Nurtured by belief, it grows,
A universe in thought composed.

Visionary Realms

Beneath the shade of ancient trees,
A labyrinth of dreams conceived.
Visionary realms unfurl,
Where mortal man and spirit twirl.

Whispered winds so softly croon,
Of future days and silver moons.
Horizon stretching far and sheer,
Meeting minds both wide and clear.

Each realm a portal, bright and vast,
To futures clear or fleeting past.
In every eye, a story gleams,
And worlds created from our dreams.

Seeds of Creation

In soil rich with endless thought,
Are seeds of creation softly wrought.
Each idea planted deep,
In the mind, they gently sleep.

They burgeon forth in moments keen,
With colors bold and sights unseen.
From silent ground they break and grow,
Reaching for a sky they know.

Tended with imagination's grace,
They flourish into dreams embraced.
Seeds of vision, grand and bright,
Bloom into endless realms of light.

Mind's Palette

A canvas wide, the mind's vast shore,
With hues and shades forever more.
The brush of thought sweeps far and wide,
Creating worlds where dreams abide.

Each stroke a vision, bold and pure,
In colors rich and textures sure.
From dawn to dusk the artistry,
Reveals a boundless mystery.

Ideas blend to form a scene,
In tones both bright and serene.
On mind's palette, truth and lore,
Are painted lives forevermore.

Embers of Thought

In twilight's silent glow,
Whispers of ideas start to grow,
From mind's vast, deep expanse,
Embers of thought take a chance.

Dreams ignite with silent flair,
Phantoms dance in evening air,
Echoes of the unseen past,
Through shadows, they are cast.

Contemplations softly blaze,
Wisps of hope in warmest haze,
Flickers of a future bright,
In the quiet of the night.

Infinite Horizons

Beyond the hills, where dawn breaks free,
Endless skies embrace the sea,
Horizons stretch so wide and vast,
Promises of journeys past.

Stars above, in endless dance,
Waves below, in mystic trance,
Paths unseen by human eye,
Boundless realms we're drawn to try.

Through the mist of morning light,
Dreams ascend to daring height,
Infinite, the road ahead,
With every step, our spirits led.

Symphony of Sparks

In the forge where metals blend,
Crafted by the hands of men,
Sparks leap high in graceful arcs,
Birth of a symphony of sparks.

Hammer's rhythm, anvil's beat,
Creating beauty, indiscreet,
Each strike a note, each flame a song,
In this space where they belong.

From molten core, to steel refined,
Artistry and strength combined,
A symphony, through toil and fire,
Resonates with fierce desire.

Genesis of Innovation

From a seed of simple thought,
New creation thus is wrought,
Innovation's humble spark,
Ignites in minds, bright and stark.

Boundaries shift, break and bend,
Ideas form and then transcend,
A genesis in every start,
Pulled from depths of human heart.

In the light of curious eyes,
Wonders wake and visions rise,
Future shaped by dreams once small,
Innovation's call to all.

Mind's Palette

In the quiet of the night,
Where thoughts weave and churn,
Colors merge in silent flight,
As moonlit visions burn.

Hues of dreams yet to be,
Brushstrokes of the past,
Canvas spread beneath the sea,
Where time is always fast.

Echoes form in mystic shades,
Whispers from the heart,
Memories that never fade,
A perfect work of art.

Vibrant Muse

In fields of golden light,
A muse dances free,
Her whispers ignite,
The flames of poetry.

With each step she weaves,
Threads of vibrant hue,
Between the autumn leaves,
Painting skies anew.

Through valleys deep and wide,
She casts her brilliant spell,
Guiding hearts to confide,
In the tales they tell.

Song of the Soul

Under a twilight sky,
The soul begins to sing,
A melody that flies,
On ever-changing wings.

Notes of joy and sorrow,
Haunting and profound,
Echoes of tomorrow,
In each lilting sound.

Binding hearts together,
In harmony and grace,
Through storms and gentle weather,
Time cannot displace.

Unfurling Marvels

Beneath the morning sun,
Marvels start to bloom,
Day's journey just begun,
Dispelling night's gloom.

Petals soft and fair,
Unfold in bright array,
Spreading in the air,
The dawn of a new day.

Wonders yet unseen,
In nature's quiet scheme,
A world forever green,
Unraveled in a dream.

Flight of Fancy

In skies of dreams, I rise so high,
Riding winds where stars do lie.
Whispers of clouds, secrets they sigh,
Wings of imagination, I fly.

Golden beams of dawn break light,
Chasing shadows from the night.
Above the world, my spirit bright,
Colouring the void, my heart takes flight.

Echoes of laughter fill the air,
In this realm, all burdens pare.
Boundless and free without a care,
Endless skies my soul does wear.

Moments fleeting, in twilight's hue,
Painting rainbows, bright and true.
Held aloft by visions new,
Thoughts and dreams together flew.

Far beyond where eyes can see,
A tapestry of possibility.
Unfurling wings of purest glee,
The journey's song, my fantasy.

Luminescent Thoughts

In the depth of silent night,
Came a spark, a glowing light.
Ideas dance in pure delight,
Mind alight with endless might.

Whispers of the moon's tender kiss,
Each thought shimmering in bliss.
Silvery trails in the abyss,
Moments of eternal reminisce.

Glowing embers, wisdom's flare,
Crystals of dreams linger there.
Hope and wonder gently share,
Weaving tales in moonlit air.

Stars align in serendipity,
Charting paths of life's decree.
Through the veil of mystery,
Clusters of ideas set free.

Brilliance coursing through my veins,
Guided by illumined reins.
Every spark in time remains,
Echoes of light within my brains.

Sculpting the Abstract

Crafting forms from empty space,
Lines and curves, an artist's grace.
Shaping realms without a trace,
Epochs whisper in the chase.

Hands decipher silent codes,
Patterns where creation nodes.
Vital essence deftly modes,
In abstract realms, the spirit bodes.

Metaphors of time and air,
Ideas solid in their lair.
Chiseling thoughts with tender care,
Forms arise, distinct and rare.

Worlds emerge from shadows cast,
A mosaic of the present and past.
Creativity's spell tightly clasped,
Every stroke a universe vast.

In the flux of shape and void,
Imagination fully deployed.
Dreams and visions intertwined,
Crafting abstracts undefined.

Essence of Creativity

In the heart of inspiration's flame,
Lies a force none can tame.
Ideas birthing without name,
Essence pure, an endless game.

Whispers of a muse's sigh,
Breath of thought beneath the sky.
In each moment, visions fly,
Crafting wonders, mind's reply.

Palette of emotions blend,
Where reality and dreams suspend.
Every start and every end,
Fertile ground where thoughts extend.

Harmony in chaos found,
Concepts lifting off the ground.
Inspiration's silent sound,
In the soul, ideas unbound.

Creating worlds with every stroke,
Wisps of fancies gently stoke.
Flame of passion we invoke,
Essence of creativity, we evoke.

Heartbeat of Ideas

In silence, thoughts are born anew,
A realm where whispers turn to hue,
Where every pulse ignites a flame,
And dreams and reality are one and the same.

A moment's beat, a spark divine,
Connections form in heart and mind,
In the void where chaos reigns,
Insight's light a mind unchains.

With every beat, a rhythm flows,
A current where new wisdom grows,
Boundless, wild, it's ever free,
Ideas dance like waves at sea.

Each heartbeat marks a new creation,
Ideas rise from inspiration,
Merging thoughts both old and new,
Creating visions that ensue.

Guided not by sight alone,
But by the pulse of thoughts unknown,
From mind to heart and back they weave,
The fabric of the world they cleave.

Muse in Motion

The muse, she dances through the air,
With grace that banishes despair,
Her whispers fuel the artist's hand,
In silent rhythms through the land.

Each step she takes, a world transforms,
Through colors wild and tempests warm,
In motion constant, she bestows,
A gift where endless beauty flows.

Can't catch her gaze, she's fleeting fast,
Fleeting, yet her touch will last,
Through time and space, she weaves her spell,
An endless wellspring, wishes quell.

Her motion sparks a brilliant blaze,
In canvas, stone, or poet's phrase,
The fleeting touch, on heart it stays,
A muse in motion never sways.

Ephemeral and yet so clear,
A force that artists hold so dear,
With every move, she breathes anew,
A muse in motion, swift and true.

Kaleidoscope Vision

Gaze deep within the turning glass,
A world of colors come to pass,
Fragmented light reclaims its form,
In patterns woven, ever warm.

A dance of hues, a prism's play,
Transcending night, embracing day,
Each turn reveals a new delight,
A symphony of shape and light.

The vision spins, a rhythmic flow,
A world within, where dreams bestow,
Infinite in their grand array,
In kaleidoscope, thoughts sway.

With every glance, a story told,
In shifting hues and threads of gold,
A universe of endless sight,
Within its depths, pure delight.

Boundless realms through crystals known,
In mirrored fragments, truth is shown,
Kaleidoscope, a vision clear,
Where vibrant worlds draw us near.

Symphony of Thought

Within the quiet of the mind,
A symphony of thoughts aligned,
Where melodies of insight play,
In harmonies that gently sway.

Each note, a spark of pure design,
Thoughts intertwined in perfect line,
From silence, music's force unbound,
In inner realms, it's ever found.

A cadence found in whispered dreams,
In measures soft, like flowing streams,
The orchestra within, it sings,
A chorus born from wisdom's springs.

In stillness where the soul reflects,
The symphony of thought connects,
A timeless dance in mental space,
In every heart, it finds its place.

Through crescendos and soft refrains,
The melody in thought remains,
A symphony both bold and wise,
A song where endless wonders rise.

Pioneering Visions

In quest of dreams that soar high,
Beyond the seen, to the sky,
We trek through realms uncharted,
With fervent hearts, undaunted.

Every frontier we embrace,
New wonders in time and space,
With courage as our guiding star,
We venture forth, near and far.

Together we shall pave the way,
In the light of a brighter day,
In unity and grand design,
Our pioneering visions shine.

Boundaries fade, horizons gleam,
In the pursuit of every dream,
As guardians of the future's lore,
We are the dreamers, evermore.

Celestial Impressions

Beneath the stars' eternal gleam,
We float within a cosmic dream,
Where galaxies and nebulae,
Whisper secrets of the sky.

The constellations paint the night,
With stories ancient, pure delight,
A tapestry of endless light,
Guiding travelers' silent flight.

In moonlit glow and solar rays,
The universe, in varied ways,
Speaks to hearts as old as time,
In melodies without a rhyme.

We gaze in awe, with eyes aglow,
At wonders far we long to know,
Celestial tunes, impressions deep,
In cosmic tales, our spirits steep.

Brush with Enchantment

On canvas wide, with colors rare,
An artist's dream, beyond compare,
With every stroke, a magic touch,
The world transforms, as such.

A whisper of the mystic's light,
To shadows cast, from day to night,
The brush does dance in rhythmic grace,
Infusing charm in empty space.

In hues of dawn and twilight's glow,
The winds of wonder gently flow,
Each painting breathes with life anew,
A glimpse of what could be, and true.

In the gallery of heart and mind,
A touch of magic we can find,
With brush and spirit intertwined,
Enchanting worlds, forever kind.

Awakening Reveries

In the quiet of the dawn's first light,
Dreams take flight, a wondrous sight,
Awakening from silver sleep,
To promises the morning keeps.

Whispers of the day begin,
In gentle hues on nature's skin,
A symphony of life replays,
In the tender, warming rays.

With each moment passing slow,
Reveries in hearts do grow,
In the dance of time's embrace,
Every breath a sweet retrace.

In the garden of the mind,
A thousand blossoms intertwined,
Awakened by the morning's kiss,
In reveries of boundless bliss.

Unseen Orchestra

In whispers of the dawn, they play,
Invisible, their symphonies sway.
Notes of morning, softly blend,
Harmonies in shadows send.

A gentle breeze, the strings do pluck,
Birdsongs in chorus, finches cluck.
Leaves as cymbals, rustling sound,
Nature's stage where dreams are found.

Raindrops tap like tiny drums,
Echoes of what is yet to come.
Thunder rolls in distant roar,
Percussion of a storm’s encore.

Moonlight's glow, a flute so clear,
Weaves through night, a melody dear.
Stars like chimes in sparkling flight,
An unseen orchestra of the night.

Each creature adds its special part,
To this concert of the heart.
Quiet moments filled with grace,
Music in the hidden space.

Quill of the Sage

Ink flows from wisdom’s well,
Stories ancient, secrets dwell.
Pages whisper, truths unfold,
Legends from the days of old.

A quill dipped in mystic light,
Scribes the lore of endless night.
Woven tales of gods and men,
Inscribe the now, recount the then.

Parables that guide the lost,
Words weighed without a cost.
Scribing answers to the quest,
Every line a soul’s request.

In twilight's glow, the sage will pen,
Mysteries for the seeking men.
Verses etched in timeless prose,
Where destiny and wisdom close.

Though the ink may fade someday,
The quill’s resolve shall light the way.
Through the epochs, whispers age,
Tales inscribed by quill of sage.

Threads of Fantasy

Weave the dreams in silken threads,
Fantasy where vision spreads.
Kingdoms born of hope and light,
Wanderers of the endless night.

Dragons soar in skies ablaze,
Knights in armor, valiant craze.
Fairies dance in forest glades,
Magic blooms in evening's shade.

Quests of old and futures bright,
Heroes on their epic flight.
Sorcery and spells entwine,
Myths and wonders so divine.

Castles loom in misty veils,
Ships that sail on fabled gales.
Lands of wonder, skies of blue,
Fantasy where dreams come true.

So stitch by stitch our tales are spun,
On the loom of setting sun.
Every thread a story weaves,
In the tapestry of dreams believed.

Celestial Imagining

Stars align in cosmic dance,
Galaxies in vast expanse.
Spirals twirl in silent grace,
Universe, a boundless place.

Planets spin in stardust rings,
Moons align with cosmic strings.
Nebulas of colors blend,
Celestial dreams that never end.

Shooting stars, they blaze afar,
Whispers from a distant star.
Constellations map the night,
Guiding sailors in their flight.

Black holes weave their mystery,
Portals to eternity.
Darkness hides the light within,
Secrets of the astral spin.

In the void, where dreams are born,
Tales of suns and stars adorn.
Celestial musings softly sing,
Echoes of imagining.

Horizon of Thoughts

On the edge where dreams reside,
Imagination stretches wide,
Beyond the realm of night and day,
Thoughts like stars light the way.

Waves of wonder gently crash,
Ideas form in brilliant flash,
Paths unknown invite the mind,
Wisdom's treasure there to find.

Skies of endless inspiration,
Guide us toward our aspiration,
Mystic winds of change appear,
Whisper secrets to the ear.

Journey through the twilight mist,
Hopes and visions coexist,
Ephemeral, yet ever bright,
Thoughts converge in gentle light.

On horizons far and vast,
Time dissolves, mere shadows cast,
In the space where notions gleam,
We voyage forth on streams of dream.

Wellspring of Brilliance

A fountain flows from deep within,
Kindling the spark of wit and kin,
In quiet depths, a hidden source,
Gives life to thought with boundless force.

Glimmering in sunlight's grace,
Mirroring a timeless place,
Drops of wisdom freely swirl,
Into the mind, ideas unfurl.

Infinite, the wellspring's gift,
Causing hearts and minds to lift,
Through reflection, insight grown,
A brilliance, uniquely known.

Cascading waves of silent truth,
Speak to both the sage and youth,
In each ripple, knowledge thrives,
Feeding dreams where brilliance dives.

Let us drink from this pure stream,
Awaken to a brighter dream,
For in the brilliance, we shall find,
A wellspring for the heart and mind.

Pulse of Genius

Beneath the calm of ceaseless thought,
A vibrant pulse is keenly sought,
Rhythms of the mind's embrace,
Creating wonders, leaving trace.

In every beat, a spark ignites,
Illuminating darkest nights,
A cadence pure, of genius bold,
With every throb, new worlds unfold.

Echoes of a heart's desire,
A symphony of inner fire,
Intuition, insight's friend,
Guiding us to wisdom's end.

Pulsing wave of conscious draw,
Breaking through convention's law,
In the genius pulse we trust,
From the dust, to brilliance thrust.

Listen to the rhythmic song,
Where heart and mind and soul belong,
For in that pulse, we truly see,
The boundless depths of mystery.

Seeds of Innovation

Planted deep in fertile ground,
Ideas in silence, gather round,
Nurtured by a curious mind,
New creations we shall find.

As the sun of vision gleams,
Awakening our wildest dreams,
Tender shoots begin to rise,
In the garden of the wise.

With each thought, a seed is sown,
Into forests, they have grown,
Branches stretch to unknown skies,
Bearing fruits that pierce disguise.

Winds of change will softly blow,
Helping seeds of wonder grow,
In the bloom of innovation,
We discover a new foundation.

Ever-green, the seeds shall be,
Roots of possibility,
For in their growth, we joyously see,
The future shaped by you and me.

Boundless Muse

In endless realms of thought we roam,
Where dreams and whispers find their home.
A spark ignites the silent night,
Unveils the dawn with pure delight.

Through shadowed woods, past ancient trees,
The boundless muse sets spirits free.
With quill in hand, we dance and weave,
Our souls entwined in what we believe.

A canvas vast, with hues unknown,
A symphony of hearts and tone.
Stars above, like guiding fire,
Lead us through the endless choir.

Each verse a beacon through the dark,
Each word a flame, a vivid spark.
In boundless skies, our spirits rise,
All dreams beneath the same vast skies.

Veins of Gold

Beneath the earth, in shadows cold,
Lie hidden veins of precious gold.
A silent force, a story told,
In ancient rocks, so brave and bold.

For every dream that's held aloft,
There's treasure deep, yet held so soft.
A promise gleams in every stone,
A silent heart, a golden throne.

Within the earth, life whispers low,
In veins of gold, the secrets flow.
The waters spring, with tales of old,
In rivers bright, the dreams unfold.

What once was dark now shines anew,
As veins of gold breathe skies of blue.
In every heart, a spark's conceived,
In every soul, a dream believed.

Eternal Muse

Across the span of time's wide sea,
Lies an eternal muse, wild and free.
In every age, in every heart,
A whispered call, a work of art.

In ancient scrolls, in modern prose,
Eternal muse in silence flows.
From distant stars to earthly climes,
It weaves its tale through endless rhymes.

Through every tear, through every smile,
The muse endures, through every trial.
An endless dance, a timeless song,
It binds the world where dreams belong.

For every soul that dares to see,
The muse is there, in you, in me.
We pen our lives, in verses pure,
With every line, the muse endures.

Dreamweaver's Touch

In twilight's embrace, where shadows play,
The Dreamweaver touches night and day.
With threads of stars, and whispers soft,
They weave the dreams that carry us aloft.

In silent hours, when the world is still,
Their magic stirs, our hearts to fill.
A tapestry of wonder spun,
Beneath the moon, begun, undone.

Through realms unseen, through time’s embrace,
The Dreamweaver’s touch leaves not a trace.
Yet in our hearts, the dreams reside,
A world of secrets tucked inside.

When morning breaks, the spell will wane,
But in our souls, the dreams remain.
With every dawn, a touch so light,
Dreamweaver’s gifts, from night to night.

Silent Inspiration

In the hush of morning's rise,
Dreams coalesce in azure skies.
Whispers of the dawn ignite,
Silent muse in golden light.

Words unspoken softly gleam,
Filling hearts with hope and dream.
Nature's breath, in silence found,
Crafts a world where love is bound.

Twilight fades, the stars alight,
Guiding souls with gentle might.
Inspiration, silent, clear,
In the calm, we hold it near.

Infinite Plenitude

Vast expanse, horizon's blend,
Where the skies and waters mend.
Endless seas of cosmic hue,
Infinite, serene, and true.

Stars like jewels, brilliant bright,
Pierce the canvas of the night.
Time suspended, boundless flow,
Gifts of wonder gently sow.

Every breath, a universe,
Infinite, no end, no curse.
We, the whispers of the vast,
Infinite, entwined, and cast.

Awash in Wonder

Burning hues of sunrise greet,
Hearts in rhythm, softly beat.
Nature’s canvas, broad and grand,
Painted with a master’s hand.

Mysteries in shadows hide,
Lurking by the ocean's tide.
Whispers carried on the breeze,
Set the spirit’s soul at ease.

Eyes behold the world anew,
Bathed in light of every hue.
Awash in wonder, spirits soar,
Seeking beauty, evermore.

Gems of Insight

In the quiet, thoughts align,
Gems of insight, rare and fine.
Within the mind's vast, deep sea,
Truth and wisdom, wild and free.

Clarity in silence blooms,
Banishing the darkest glooms.
In the stillness, knowledge grows,
Light within, it softly glows.

Every challenge, every plight,
Leads us to these gems of light.
Insight shines through night and day,
Guiding us upon our way.

Within the Canvas

Upon the canvas streaked with hues,
Imagination wildly fused.
Brushstrokes dance with vibrant grace,
In colors life they do embrace.

A whisper of the artist's soul,
In every line a story whole.
Layered dreams in sunlight's gleam,
A painted world, a silent dream.

Each blend of shade, a heartbeat's call,
In shadows rise, in highlights fall.
Palette whispers truths untold,
In pigments lie both young and old.

Echoes of Genius

In the quiet of the night,
Brilliance sparks its first light.
Genius wanders boundless skies,
Seeds of thought in darkness rise.

Mind a labyrinth vast and wide,
Where echoes of the past reside.
Whispers faint, yet deeply clear,
In each thought, a world appears.

Bright ideas, like morning sun,
Break through veil, embracing dawn.
In the corridors of mind,
Treasures of the soul we find.

Awakened Dreams

In slumber's grasp, dreams come alive,
Where fantasies and wishes thrive.
Uncharted realms by night revealed,
In quiet minds, true hope concealed.

Wings of thought begin to soar,
To distant lands, to foreign shores.
Within this realm, we dare to be,
The truest self where dreams run free.

As dawn's first light begins to break,
From dreams we rise, anew, awake.
With hearts inspired and spirits high,
Awakened dreams now touch the sky.

Ignite the Soul

Beneath the stars where fires gleam,
Lies the power to dream extreme.
Passions flare in endless night,
Guided by that burning light.

In each heartbeat, courage found,
In every breath, a silent sound.
Fuel the spirit, fan the flame,
To greatness soar, to destiny's name.

With fervor strong, our paths we mold,
Through trials vast and courage bold.
Let the spark of life ignite,
And guide the soul through endless light.

Canvas of Dreams

In twilight's gentle, silent sweep,
Brushstrokes dance, the world asleep.
Colors blend in midnight gleams,
Painting vibrant, whispered dreams.

Stars align on velvet skies,
Hopes and wishes softly rise.
Each stroke a story, old and new,
Created where the heart is true.

Fantasies on canvas thread,
Tales of joy and skies of red.
Moonlight whispers, softly beams,
Crafting realms of endless dreams.

Echoes from the artist's heart,
Forms a world, a work of art.
Silent musings, inward streams,
Flow into the canvas, dreams.

Brushes lead where spirits seek,
Secrets told in colors meek.
Dreams awoken, gently teems,
On the canvas, life redeems.

Radiance of Thought

In the stillness of the night,
Thoughts arise, pure and bright.
Ideas bloom in slender ties,
Radiance found in the skies.

Minds engaged in silent dance,
Intellect and light enhance.
Every spark, a newborn star,
Guiding us both near and far.

Wisdom born from quiet spaces,
Reaching forth to unknown places.
Light of knowledge softly caught,
Radiates from every thought.

Stars of brilliance, paths unfold,
Endless stories to be told.
Mystery and insight sought,
In the radiance of thought.

Dreams ignited by a spark,
Guiding light within the dark.
Every whisper, every taught,
Illuminates our radiant thought.

Embers of Genius

Deep within the quiet night,
Burns a glow, an inner light.
Whispers of the creative stream,
Embers bright with wild dream.

From the depths, bright passions glow,
Inner fires start to grow.
Each idea a blazing ember,
Sparks of genius to remember.

Courage found in quiet muse,
Lighting paths we rarely choose.
Flames of insight start to spread,
Filling voids within our head.

Ignite the mind with vibrant flare,
Creativity beyond compare.
Embers warm and visions grand,
Built from dreams at mind's command.

Echoes from the inner flight,
Genius shines in darkest night.
Every ember, every beam,
Kindles life within the dream.

Whispered Wonders

In the hushed and silent air,
Whispers float, a gentle prayer.
Nature's wonders softly call,
Magic spans both great and small.

Trees converse in rustled leaves,
Echoes through the golden eves.
Secrets told from dusk till dawn,
Voices fade in morning's yawn.

Rivers murmur words of old,
Mysteries in currents bold.
Mountains stand with stories grand,
Whispered truths in every land.

Starlit nights and twilight's sigh,
Veil of wonder in the sky.
Glimmering tales from distant stars,
Tell of worlds beyond the bars.

Silent notes on gentle breeze,
Whispered wonders through the trees.
Nature's symphony takes flight,
In the wonder of the night.

Carved by Dreams

In the quiet hush of midnight's gleam,
Whispered tales, a twilight theme,
Shapes are born, surreal and grand,
Carved by dreams, a mystical hand.

Through shadows deep, across the mind,
Visions fleeting, hard to find,
Etched in silver, moonlit beams,
Life unfurls in twilight streams.

Stars align in cosmic flight,
Guiding souls through endless night,
Each a fragment, stories weaved,
In the silence, hearts perceived.

Paths untrodden, futures bright,
In the dark, we find our light,
Every hope and wildest scheme,
Crafted finely, carved by dreams.

Comet Trails of Thought

Across the sky, in cosmic sweep,
Ideas dance, where minds do leap,
Glittering threads of light they've caught,
Are comet trails of boundless thought.

In the void, where silence sings,
Wisdom flies on angel's wings,
Flashing bright through darkest night,
Igniting minds with pure insight.

In patterns bold and wild they trace,
Wonder’s realm in endless space,
Each a spark in night’s expanse,
A cosmic symphony of chance.

Their passage marks the unseen thread,
Of thoughts unspoken, softly spread,
Crafted lights in silence brought,
Ephemeral, these trails of thought.

Panoramic Vistas

Horizons stretch in gilded hues,
Under vast, unending views,
Nature's brush in colors plays,
A masterpiece in dawning rays.

Mountains high and valleys wide,
Oceans deep in tranquil tide,
Skies adorned in painted skies,
Whispering of wild surmise.

Rolling hills and forests dense,
Each a tale of consequence,
River's course and desert's span,
Part of life's eternal plan.

Every glance, a story told,
In the daylight’s touch of gold,
Panoramic vistas weave,
Dreamlike wonder to believe.

Odes to Beginnings

In the stillness, where dawn breaks free,
New beginnings call to thee,
A canvas soft, with morning's light,
Dreams take flight, in infinite height.

Whispers of the breezes sing,
Promises of what they bring,
Buds that bloom, the first snowfall,
Each new start, an endless thrall.

Steps are taken, hearts anew,
Journeys vast in every view,
Life's mosaic, freshly spun,
Moments start as one by one.

Time, it marches, yet we see,
Beauty in what's yet to be,
In the present, future gleams,
Odes to beginnings, like new dreams.

Beyond the Horizon

The sun dips low, a golden flight,
Beyond the hills, escapes the night,
Stars awaken, with whispered gleam,
A tranquil sea, a sailor's dream.

The winds of change begin to blow,
Across the skies, a scarlet show,
Mountains whisper ancient tales,
Of timeless paths and hidden trails.

A bird in flight, with wings so wide,
Glides through air, with strength and pride,
Chasing dreams and boundless skies,
Through realms unseen, where freedom lies.

In twilight's glow, the shadows dance,
Leaves rustle in a silent trance,
Oceans hum a soothing tune,
Beneath the watchful, crescent moon.

Beyond the horizon, wonders lie,
In every star, in every sigh,
A world of magic, pure and bright,
Awaits us at the edge of night.

Seeds of Brilliance

In fertile soil, hopes are sown,
With tender care, and love they've grown,
Each tiny seed, a dream so bright,
Reaching upwards, seeking light.

Raindrops fall, with gentlest kiss,
Nature's grace, a tender bliss,
Roots spread wide, in silent quest,
Drawing strength for future tests.

Sunlight warms the budding leaves,
In a world where spirit weaves,
Colors burst with life serene,
A tapestry of vibrant green.

Whispers of the morning breeze,
Tickle branches, bend the trees,
In their dance, they tell a tale,
Of strength and grace that won't derail.

Seeds of brilliance, potent bloom,
Scatter light, dispel the gloom,
In every heart, a garden grows,
Where boundless inspiration flows.

Dance of Imagination

In shadows cast by daylight's end,
A world of dreams begins to bend,
Where fantasies take root and grow,
With endless skies in vibrant glow.

Colors swirl in liquid streams,
A kaleidoscope of boundless dreams,
Mountains soar and rivers bend,
In realms where time can lapse and mend.

The air is thick with whispered sight,
As stories bloom in velvet night,
Creatures born of thought take flight,
In a dance of pure delight.

Wisps of moonlight paint the beams,
Of fairy dust and childhood schemes,
Each whispered hope, a vivid spark,
Igniting life within the dark.

Dance of imagination wide,
Where wonders drift on every tide,
In this realm of thoughts set free,
A universe of possibility.

Colors of Thought

In the canvas of the mind's expanse,
Ideas flicker, whirl, and dance,
Brush strokes of a vibrant hue,
Craft a world that's always new.

Concepts bloom in abstract form,
A symphony where dreams are born,
Patterns shift in fluid lines,
A masterpiece through shifting times.

Shades of reason, tones of grace,
Paint the contours of this space,
In every hue, a story lies,
Woven in with truth and lies.

A palette rich with life's detail,
Moments captured, thoughts unveiled,
Each color speaks a silent word,
A silent song yet softly heard.

Colors of thought, a grand display,
Invites the mind to dream, to play,
In this realm where vision grows,
Imagination freely flows.

Serenade to Genius

In twilight's calm, the mind takes flight,
Ideas bloom in silver light.
Dreams weave strings of endless thought,
In genius' grasp, all wonder's caught.

Beyond the stars, the answers lie,
Explorers of the cosmic sky.
The pulse of time, a steady beat,
In every heart, a rhythm sweet.

Crafting worlds from mere desire,
Imagination lights the fire.
In the void, we chase the gleam,
Of brilliance born from endless dream.

Through darkest night, the visions flow,
In whispered tones, our spirits grow.
By genius touched, the world transforms,
In boundless mind, creation swarms.

For in the soul, a spark that's bright,
Lights paths unseen, within the night.
Forevermore, the quest remains,
In genius' hymn, the world sustains.

Translucent Whispers

Through veils of mist, a voice does call,
In softest tones, where shadows fall.
Translucent whispers, secrets stay,
In twilight's grasp, they gently sway.

Ethereal threads of starlit dreams,
In whispered thoughts, the silence gleams.
An echo in the quiet night,
Guides hearts toward a distant light.

In moon's embrace, the whispers spin,
A tale of love, where souls begin.
In every breath, a hidden song,
That calls to those who've wandered long.

In stillness deep, the truth unfolds,
In whispers' grace, the heart beholds.
A dance of shadows, soft and pure,
Through whispers' veil, our souls endure.

In silent nights, the whispers find,
The chambers of the open mind.
Translucent whispers, ever fair,
A gentle wind within the air.

Threads of Eternity

In timeless dance, the threads entwine,
Weaving lives through fate's design.
Beyond the veil of fleeting day,
The threads of eternity stay.

Each soul, a thread in cosmic loom,
Spins tales of joy, and whispers bloom.
In labyrinths of time's embrace,
We trace the lines of every face.

From dawn to dusk, the threads remain,
In sorrow's loss, and love's refrain.
A tapestry, both vast and small,
Each thread, a part, one and all.

With hands unseen, the weaver's touch,
Grants strength and grace, from little much.
In fabric worn, and colors shown,
The threads of life, a story known.

Eternal flow, through time and space,
The threads of fate, we all must face.
In unity, our spirits bind,
In threads of eternity, aligned.

Morning Epiphanies

With dawn's first light, the shadows flee,
And morning's kiss sets visions free.
Epiphanies in golden hue,
Awake the soul to something new.

The dew on grass, a fleeting gem,
Reflects the world's diadem.
In morning's breath, the whispers sing,
Of endless hope and budding spring.

Emerge and stretch, from slumber's hold,
Embrace the day, both brave and bold.
In morning's calm, the heart reveals,
The truths that night so gently seals.

Awaken to the vibrant skies,
As morning epiphanies rise.
In every ray, a promise true,
Of dreams that light the world anew.

In stillness deep, with eyes aglow,
We learn the things that mornings show.
Epiphanies in dawn's embrace,
Guide us through the endless chase.

Cradle of Thought

In twilight's gentle, silent gleam,
Whispers form the quiet stream.
Ideas dance in shadows caught,
Within the cradle of pure thought.

Unfolding dreams in colors bright,
A tapestry of endless night.
From silence springs the unseen,
A world of wonder, vast, serene.

Mind's fingers trace the unseen thread,
Where possibility is gently led.
Horizon bends to new delight,
In the stillness of the night.

Every spark and every hue,
Born from thoughts both old and new.
In this cradle, softly laid,
A universe within the shade.

In quiet contemplation's hand,
A vision blooms, vast and grand.
Each thought a star, brightly sought,
Within the cradle, minds are wrought.

Echoes of Imagination

Through corridors of airy dreams,
Echoes of imagination gleam.
They whisper secrets soft and low,
In endless ebb, in gentle flow.

Painting skies with hues of gold,
Stories bright unfold, retold.
In silent voids, creation springs,
The soul's free flight on boundless wings.

Shadows play in twilight air,
Weaving patterns rich and rare.
Every echo, every call,
A testament to wonder's thrall.

A realm where fantasy takes hold,
In echoes bright, in tales bold.
Imagination’s endless pool,
Where hearts are young and minds are cool.

In the depth of quiet thought,
Echoes of the dreams are caught.
Carving paths to worlds unknown,
Where imagination’s seeds are sown.

Quest for Brilliance

Across the seas of endless time,
A quest for brilliance, pure, sublime.
With every step a shimmer bright,
Guides the soul to boundless light.

Through valleys deep and mountains high,
Underneath the wide, clear sky.
Challenges shape the inner core,
Wisdom sought forevermore.

In the heart of silent night,
Thoughts ignite in blazing flight.
A beacon calls, a starry crest,
To ever strive, to never rest.

With courage deep, the path unfolds,
A journey rich in tales untold.
Through trials, tempests, and the storm,
Emerges brilliance, freshly formed.

Upon the peak where dreams ascend,
The quest finds its radiant end.
In brilliance found, so boldly wrought,
The essence of the brilliant sought.

Labyrinth of Creation

Within the maze of thought and dream,
Creation flows, a constant stream.
A labyrinth of paths and doors,
Where imagination ever soars.

Each turn a new, mysterious way,
Where colors, shapes, and visions play.
In every curve, a story spins,
Within this maze, creation wins.

Navigating through the twisting halls,
The muse's call within them calls.
Echoes of the mind's own art,
In the labyrinth, they start.

A journey through the hidden veins,
Of creativity's ethereal plains.
Where thoughts converge and magic breeds,
A labyrinth of potent seeds.

At the center, bright and clear,
A well of endless dreams appear.
From labyrinth's heart, creation springs,
Where mind and soul together sing.

Coalesced Vision

Dreams unite in twilight's hour,
A sacred bond, a budding flower.
Fate weaves threads, fine and tight,
In shadows, blooms the purest light.

Eyes that see, hearts that know,
United paths, where rivers flow.
In silent whispers, truth unfolds,
Mysteries of the soul unrolled.

Bound by stars, our spirits dance,
In cosmic realms, a wondrous trance.
Eclipsing fears, embracing night,
Together, we ignite the light.

Hands conjoined, we paint the sky,
With hues of love, that never die.
A vision formed, in sacred craft,
Eternal bond, forever clasped.

As dawn breaks, the world awakes,
In every breath, our vision stakes.
We journey forth, through realms unknown,
Coalesced, our truth is shown.

Rise of the Muse

In dawn's embrace, she softly stirs,
A muse awakes, in whispers, purrs.
With grace and light, she takes her flight,
In mortal hearts, her beauty blurs.

From shadows deep, to peaks above,
She births new dreams, ignites with love.
A spark of hope, a gleam of fire,
In every soul, she plants desire.

Her touch is light, yet firm and true,
Awakens all to purpose new.
With every breath, she fuels the flame,
In hearts renewed, she stakes her claim.

In stories told, and songs well sung,
Her legacy, on every tongue.
Through art and dance, she lifts our eyes,
Transcending bounds, she makes us rise.

As day gives way to night's embrace,
Her spirit lingers, leaves her trace.
In dreams we chase, in visions clear,
The muse awakens, always near.

Ever-Bright Muse

In shadows cast by twilight's veil,
A muse emerges, bold and frail.
Her light, a beacon, through the night,
Guides wandering hearts to purest sight.

She sings of stars, their timeless lore,
Of oceans vast and skies that soar.
With every note, she stirs the soul,
Unwritten fates, she helps unroll.

Through sorrow's depth and joy's ascent,
Her whispers lead where hopes are spent.
A gentle hand, a tender spark,
She kindles flames within the dark.

In poets' quill and painter's brush,
Her spirit moves, with gentle hush.
From silent thoughts to loud refrain,
In every heart, she leaves her stain.

Though time may fade and seasons change,
Her light endures, beyond the range.
An ever-bright muse, eternal spark,
In her we find our way through dark.

Echoes in Silence

In stillness deep, where shadows lie,
Whispers float, like gentle sighs.
Unheard tales, in quiet weeps,
Echoes rise from silence deep.

Beneath the stars, in moonlit glow,
Silent secrets softly flow.
Unseen hands, in twilight grey,
Shape the night, in subtle sway.

Dreams unfold in muted hues,
Silent dawns where hope renews.
Through the void, with tender grace,
Echoes fill the empty space.

In silent halls of memory,
Lingers sweet, a symphony.
Notes that play, in hearts confined,
Echoes of the silence, bind.

When words are still, and breath is slow,
In silence, truths begin to grow.
Listen close, and you will find,
Echoes in the silence, kind.

Cosmic Brushstrokes

Under the night’s vast umbra, stars do weave,
A nearly silent song they cleave,
Onto the void’s pure canvas, bright they cleave,
With hues that mortals scarce believe.

Galaxies in swirls, in swathes allure,
Each dot a story, ancient and pure,
With strokes of light, the cosmos procure,
A masterpiece in dark obscure.

Nebulas like dreams, ether’s embrace,
Patterns uncharted, shadows trace,
Each spark a wish, in silent grace,
A cosmic art we long to place.

The moon whispers secrets, soft and low,
With silvery strokes, a gentle glow,
In this celestial show, the stars bestow,
An artist's rapture in the sky’s tableau.

Waves of time, through space they sweep,
In patterns vast, endless and deep,
Cosmic brushstrokes make heavens weep,
As through the stars our souls do leap.

Resplendent Murmurs

In shadows cast, the whispers gleam,
Unveiling truths within a dream,
Softly sung on a twilight stream,
Resplendent murmurs, whispers of the unseen.

By night’s embrace, they gently call,
Through silent woods, where shadows fall,
A heart’s echo, both great and small,
Resplendent murmurs, voices enthrall.

In dawn’s first blush, the light does break,
The silent hum of day’s awake,
With every sigh, the world does shake,
Resplendent murmurs, soft waves they take.

The rain that falls, a whispered plea,
In every drop, a secret key,
Unlocking dreams from sky to sea,
Resplendent murmurs, of what could be.

In lovers' eyes, a subtle sound,
In touch and glance, emotions found,
The world spins gently all around,
Resplendent murmurs, hearts unbound.

Fluttering Reveries

In meadows vast, where dreams do soar,
Butterflies dance, and spirits explore,
Their wings like whispers, evermore,
Fluttering reveries, they silently implore.

Through fragrant blooms, they gently weave,
A tapestry of hopes they leave,
With every flutter, they softly deceive,
Fluttering reveries, twilight’s eve.

In sunlit beams, their colors play,
A ballet of light, in golden sway,
Each moment a wish, by night or day,
Fluttering reveries, guiding the way.

On zephyr’s breath, their song is spun,
In every hue, life's threads are won,
A dance of souls, under the sun,
Fluttering reveries, where hearts are one.

By moon's soft glow, they find their rest,
In nature’s palm, a tranquil nest,
Dreams entwined, in cosmic fest,
Fluttering reveries, eternally blessed.

Glimmers of Enlightenment

In shadows' wake, the light does rise,
A beacon strong beyond disguise,
Enlightenment glimmers in our eyes,
A dawn unbound, to realize.

On paths untrod, where wisdom seeps,
Through whispers of the night that creeps,
In every heart, a soul that leaps,
Glimmers of enlightenment, the spirit keeps.

Through seasons' change, we journey far,
With each new dawn, a guiding star,
In every breath, a whispered scar,
Glimmers of enlightenment, where dreams are.

In silence found, a truth profound,
In quiet moments, peace is crowned,
With every step, new ground is found,
Glimmers of enlightenment, all around.

Within us lies the endless light,
A spark that breaks the darkest night,
In every soul, a flame so bright,
Glimmers of enlightenment, pure and right.

Sacred Reveries

In twilight’s tender, quiet embrace,
Whispers of stars adorn the sky,
The moon's soft glow, a lover’s face,
Guides the dreams as night drifts by.

In the hush, a sacred reverie,
Where souls converse in silent choir,
Time slows, and hearts feel unafraid,
Wrapped in the warmth of divine fire.

Beneath the canopy of endless night,
The world’s true essence is revealed,
In moments hushed by love’s pure light,
Our weary spirits gently healed.

Enigmatic Sparks

Within the forest deep and dark,
Lies secrets old and wisdom stark,
Where shadows play and whispers hark,
An ember glows, an enigmatic spark.

The wind's soft sigh, the branches sway,
A dance of echoes far away,
In twilight's realm where shadows stray,
Mysteries unfold, they say.

Between the leaves, the light thus weaves,
Tales of yore the night receives,
In whispered tones and flowing streams,
A world of hidden, boundless dreams.

Mystical Reflections

On mirrored lakes where silence lives,
The world reflects, the soul forgives,
Each ripple tells a tale of past,
A moment's glance, too soon to last.

Beneath the sky in twilight's tear,
The night begins to draw us near,
A world reborn in shadows cast,
Mystical reflections, vast.

The stars above, a silent choir,
Each spark a dream, each night a fire,
In stillness found, an endless grace,
Reflections of a peaceful place.

Notions of Fire

In the heart of night, a flame ignites,
A beacon bright in endless nights,
Notions of fire that fueled the fight,
Carved in the canvas of the night.

Through realms unseen, it waltzes free,
A dance of light for those to see,
Boundless dreams in spirits' plea,
Awake the soul's deep reverie.

Burning bright, defying fear,
In the glow, the path grows clear,
Moments, dreams, a heart's desire,
Forged anew in notions of fire.

Tapestry of Thoughts

In the quiet of the night,
When the stars begin to fade,
Threads of dreams take flight,
In a mind's serene cascade.

Ideas weave and intertwine,
Forming patterns, intricate and grand,
A tapestry, a design divine,
Crafted by an unseen hand.

Colors blend, thoughts align,
In shadows, brilliance glows,
Each thread a tale, a sign,
Of moments that the heart bestows.

Silent whispers, secrets old,
In the fabric find their place,
Wisdom spun, stories told,
In this woven, sacred space.

As dawn approaches, light reveals,
The beauty of the thought's embrace,
A masterpiece unfolds, conceals,
The magic of the silent chase.

Genesis of Dreams

In the stillness of the night,
Whispers soft, like a breeze,
A spark ignites an inner light,
Dreams begin with gentle ease.

From the depths of slumber's cave,
Shapes and forms take their flight,
Imaginations dare, and brave,
Crafting worlds from out of sight.

In the cradle of the unknown,
Visions splendid, vivid, bloom,
Seeds of wonder, dreams sown,
Dispel the dark, dispel the gloom.

A canvas vast, the mind explores,
Uncharted realms, stars unseen,
Every dream a door implores,
Come discover what they mean.

Morning breaks, the dreams recede,
But their essence lingers on,
Fueling hearts with what they need,
Hope and light at each new dawn.

Whispers of Muse

Beneath the moon's soft glow,
In the hush of twilight's grace,
Whispers of the muse do flow,
Kissing imagination's face.

In the breeze of evening's chill,
Silent voices gently call,
A muse's touch, a quiet thrill,
Inspiration gently falls.

Words and thoughts begin to play,
Dancing on the silent breeze,
Forming verses night to day,
Creating art with gentle ease.

Each whisper, a soft embrace,
Urges dreams to life anew,
In the mind, a sacred space,
Where creativity breaks through.

Morning light, the whispers fade,
But their echoes still remain,
Fuel for the artist's parade,
Songs of muse in every strain.

Sparks of Creativity

In the silence, sparks ignite,
Tiny embers glowing bright,
From the depths of thought and night,
Creativity takes its flight.

Bursting forth, the mind's bright flare,
Colors vivid, wild, divine,
Inspiration fills the air,
A masterpiece in every line.

From the spark, a fire grows,
Warming hearts and lighting dreams,
In the artist's hand it flows,
Crafting wonder with its beams.

Brightness fuels the telling tale,
From the unknown depths inside,
Sparks become a comet's trail,
Where imaginations glide.

As the flames begin to wane,
In their glow, we cherish still,
Sparks of creativity's gain,
Lights the soul, ignites the will.

Constellations of Thought

In the fabric of the night, stars weave their tale,
Mind's eye wanders, through a cosmic trail.
Dreams align in heavens so clear,
Guiding hearts with luminance dear.

Infinite patterns, in silence they speak,
Wonders profound, in shadows we seek.
Galaxies of wisdom, beyond our sight,
Illuminating paths, through velvety night.

Whispers of knowledge, in starlight unfold,
Secrets of cosmos, in stories retold.
Constellations aligned, charting our course,
Eternal journeys, in celestial force.

Stars like beacons, in dark skies they rest,
Mapping the voyage, in cosmic quest.
Thoughts like meteors, scattered yet bright,
Fleeting through souls, in the realms of twilight.

In the universe vast, our minds take flight,
Twined with the stars, in the silence of night.
Constellations of thought, a boundless sea,
Reflecting the depths of eternity.

Alchemy of Ideas

In the crucible of time, ideas transmute,
Echoes of dreams, in reality's pursuit.
From fragments of thoughts, a vision we forge,
In the fires of passion, where inspirations gorge.

Imagination's alchemy, a mystical blend,
Turning leaden thoughts, to gold in the end.
Horizons of minds, where visions collide,
Alchemy of ideas, where futures reside.

Through abstract mists, concepts unfurl,
Crafted in silence, like pearls in a swirl.
Experiment of thoughts, an endless creation,
Transforming the mundane, by sheer inspiration.

In the quest of wisdom, solutions elude,
In the forge of mind, their essence is imbued.
Transmuting the ordinary, to new paradigms,
Alchemy of ideas, transcending old times.

Potions of thought, mixed with care,
Revealing new perspectives, everywhere.
In the dance of ideas, our spirits ascend,
Creating with alchemy, a cosmos to mend.

Enchanted Whispers

Beneath the moon's soft, silvery sweep,
Whispers of enchantment, in the shadows creep.
Passing through leaves, in whispers they tell,
A symphony of secrets, casting a spell.

Mystic voices, from ages old,
Stories of wonder, in silence hold.
In twilight's embrace, the whispers flow,
Enchanting the night, with a gentle glow.

From the brook's melody, to the breeze's sigh,
Whispers of magic, in the night they fly.
Enchanting hearts, with timeless lore,
In their gentle echoes, we yearn for more.

Moonlit shadows, where whispers play,
In unseen realms, they softly sway.
Mysteries unfold, in their silent song,
Enchanting the dreamers, who follow along.

In the quiet of night, when the world is still,
Enchanted whispers, our spirits fill.
Guiding through realms, of dreams untold,
In their tender murmur, we find the soul.

Realm of Possibilities

In the realm where dreams take flight,
Boundless horizons, dawn with light.
Possibilities weave, in an endless skein,
Hopes unchain, like summer rain.

Through doors untouched, ambitions keen,
Realms unveil, the unseen scene.
Visions dissolve, into new realities,
Crafted in the sway, of possibilities.

Every step a journey, on paths uncharted,
Endless realms, where all dreams started.
Each choice a thread, in destiny's weave,
Realm of possibilities, in which we believe.

Imagination's winds, our sails caress,
Navigating seas, of pure finesse.
Infinite forks, in the road ahead,
Yet to be walked, paths we tread.

Within this realm, potential blooms,
In limitless skies, no dream entombs.
Realm of possibilities, endless and wide,
Unfolding the miracles, where we reside.

Instinctive Verve

Within the heart, a spark ignites,
A flame of truth, so pure, so bright.
Guiding steps with untamed might,
Through shadowed paths and deepest night.

Whispers of the ancient wind,
To primal forces we rescind.
In pulse and breath, our spirits blend,
In nature's arms, we find our end.

With fervent gaze, see worlds anew,
In every star and morning dew.
Instinct thus commands our view,
Through hidden realms and skies of blue.

In silent vows, the soul's delight,
Embarked we are on endless flight.
Beyond the bounds of day and night,
Embrace the call, our innate right.

Discoveries in ev'ry turn,
With every beat, our passions burn.
To instinct's call, we shall return,
And in its fire, our spirits yearn.

Harmonious Essence

In whispers soft, the cosmos sing,
A symphony in everything.
Through timeless dance, a boundless ring,
The essence of all life they bring.

Within the silence, melodies,
In unity, the heart decrees.
Through ebb and flow of ancient seas,
The sound of life, a gentle breeze.

Harmony transcends the form,
Through storm and calm, through peace and storm.
Within the soul, so pure and warm,
The essence of the norm transforms.

Across the stars, the harmonies,
In galaxies and light's degrees.
Their music flows as endless seas,
In every note, an endless tease.

So listen close, to echoes dear,
In every beat, a song sincere.
Harmonious essence, ever near,
The music of the spheres we hear.

Shaping the Light

In dawn's embrace, the light reveals,
Through golden strands, our sight it seals.
A canvas bright, each day conceals,
In shadows cast, the truth appeals.

In hands of time, the moments gleam,
Like rivers flow, a steady stream.
Shaping light, our grandest dream,
In every glow, life's radiant theme.

From dawn to dusk, the light we mold,
With colors vast and stories bold.
In whispered hues, our hands unfold,
The brilliance that our hearts hold.

Through prismed glass, the world refrains,
A dance of light in myriad chains.
In shaped delight, no form remains,
Each ray of light, our soul attains.

Amidst the dark, we carve the beams,
With love's intent, the vision streams.
Shaping light in endless dreams,
In glittered truth, our spirit teems.

Alchemy of Thought

In depths of mind where dreams reside,
An alchemy that none can hide.
Thoughts transform with silent guide,
In inner worlds, we so abide.

A spark of gold in mental seams,
Through shadowed depths, the spirit gleams.
Through alchemist's silent reams,
We forge the boundless realm of dreams.

Imagination’s cauldron stirs,
The mind’s elixirs, thoughts and words.
In every question, truth occurs,
A golden dawn that thought infers.

In mental realms, the landscapes change,
Through realms of thought, ideas range.
An alchemy both vast and strange,
The boundless mind our limits estrange.

So forge ahead, with thoughts refined,
In every breath, the alchemic mind.
In boundless space, the truths aligned,
Through thought, the universe designed.

Whispers of the Muse

In twilight's hue, where shadows play,
The muse's whisper starts the day.
Soft verses weave through evening's veil,
A subtle song, an ancient tale.

Stars align in cosmic dance,
Dreams arise from timeless trance.
Within the blend of dusk and dawn,
In silence, inspiration's drawn.

Winds that carry autumn's kiss,
Stir the heart with fleeting bliss.
Ephemeral as morning dew,
A vision clear, a path anew.

Each whisper holds the world's delight,
Guiding through the depths of night.
With gentle hand and ethereal touch,
The muse bestows creative rush.

In quiet moments, thoughts conspire,
To set the artist's soul on fire.
Through whispered words, the night reveals,
The spark that truth and beauty heals.

Echoes of Creation

In the silence of the eternal night,
Echoes of creation take flight.
From chaos blooms a stellar sea,
A cosmic waltz of destiny.

Galaxies form in astral threads,
Celestial whispers fill our heads.
With every star, a story told,
An endless journey to behold.

Mountains rise and rivers flow,
Life emerges, soft and slow.
Nature's canvas, vast and bright,
Painted under cosmic light.

Time's tapestry ever weaves,
Through cycles that the heart receives.
In the infinite array of space,
We find our humble, sacred place.

From stardust to a fleeting breath,
Creation's song defies all death.
With echoes in the boundless void,
Life's symphony is thus enjoyed.

Sparks of Brilliance

Morning mist on fields of gold,
Ideas bloom, the mind's unfold.
A moment's spark, a sudden flare,
In thought's embrace, we're held with care.

Lightning strikes in mental skies,
Brilliance shows in seeking eyes.
A flash of genius, bold and bright,
Illuminates the darkest night.

Inspiration, a fleeting guest,
Fires the soul, ignites the quest.
From deep within, the answers rise,
To challenges that cloud the skies.

Thoughts converge and pathways form,
In the eye of the creative storm.
Boundless realms of possibility,
Await the daring mind to see.

With every spark, a fire starts,
Igniting dreams within our hearts.
Through brilliance forged from inner gleam,
We turn our visions into theme.

Symphony of Ideas

Notes of thought in rhythmic sound,
A symphony where dreams are found.
Harmonies of light and shade,
Compose the mind's grand serenade.

Each idea a note in time,
Merging in a perfect rhyme.
Melodies of depth and grace,
Emanate from boundless space.

Chords of wisdom, threads of gold,
In the symphony, truths unfold.
Voices blend in sweet accord,
Creating beauty, self-assured.

Concepts rise in crescendos high,
Touching hearts, the spirits fly.
Through the movements, fast and slow,
The symphony's essence starts to grow.

With each measure, life's profound,
Ideas echo all around.
A symphony of endless dreams,
Flows through thought's eternal streams.

Whispered Epiphanies

In the hush of twilight's sway,
Secrets dance in muted tones,
Barely heard, yet vast and wide,
Silent truths that life condones.

Timeless echoes lightly tread,
Upon the chambers of the mind,
Whispers form the woven thread,
Of dreams and hopes intertwined.

Epiphanies in shadows glide,
Awakening the dormant thought,
Softly spoken, free to bide,
Ideas, by whispers caught.

In silence, wisdom finds its way,
To hearts and souls in need,
Where whispered secrets gently lay,
Planting inspiration's seed.

Illuminated paths appear,
As whispers softly fade,
Guiding steps with vision clear,
In twilight's gentle cascade.

Radiant Sparks

Stars ignite the velvet night,
Scattering their radiant sparks,
Guiding sailors with their light,
Through the ocean's inky arcs.

In the hearth, a fire glows,
Embodied warmth, a brilliant blaze,
Memories in ember shows,
Stories whispered, hearts amaze.

Creativity’s radiant flame,
Ignites the soul with sparks of fire,
Inspiration calls by name,
Filling life with vast desire.

Radiant dreams in amber hue,
Illuminate the darkest eve,
Painting skies with fiery queues,
In what our spirits weave.

Every thought, a glimmering spark,
In the vast expanse of night,
Guides us from within the dark,
Toward a future, ever bright.

Chasing the Muse

Through forests deep and sprawling wide,
Where muses hide 'neath verdant leaves,
In shadows where the whispers bide,
A poet's heart, in silence, grieves.

Chasing dreams that dance on air,
Elusive visions, fleeting glance,
In twilight's tender, loving care,
Creativity's soft trance.

Paths entwined with starlit threads,
Lead seekers to the twilight glade,
Where muses rest their weary heads,
In the quiet, dreams are made.

Ever chasing feathered thoughts,
Across the canvas of the mind,
In the hush of twilight wrought,
Inspiration we shall find.

Whispered words in midnight's song,
Carried on the evening breeze,
Chasing muses all night long,
Awakening the poet's pleas.

Brushstrokes of Wonder

A canvas blank, awaiting hues,
Brushstrokes dance in vibrant light,
Colors blend and gently fuse,
Creating wonder in the night.

Each stroke a whisper, bold and true,
Painting scenes of far-off lands,
In the twilight's muted blue,
Stories bloom from artist's hands.

Brushstrokes weave a world of dreams,
In every hue and every shade,
Silent tales in painter’s schemes,
On the canvas softly laid.

Wonder captured, moment’s grace,
In each brushstroke's gentle trace,
Bringing life to empty space,
With colors filling time’s embrace.

Through the dance of brush and soul,
Wonder’s light begins to shine,
Completing the artistic whole,
In the spectrum’s bright design.

Clarity’s Canvas

With brush strokes of understanding,
A world in focus, vision clear,
Painted truths in hues expanding,
Clarity draws the mind near.

On canvas bright with insight sharp,
Mysteries unveiled, pure art,
Each detail etched, not left apart,
Revealing wisdom to the heart.

Colors vivid in thought's expanse,
Balancing darkness with the light,
In the dance of reason’s chance,
Truths and wonders in plain sight.

Harmony sings in disciplined grace,
Proportions just, perspective sound,
In each fine line, a quiet space,
Where clarity and thought abound.

From dawn to dusk in quiet toil,
The canvas grows with dreams unfurled,
In every shape, in every coil,
Clarity’s vision shapes the world.

Timeless Dreamscapes

In realms where time itself does sleep,
Dreamscapes vast and silent grow,
Uncharted paths in memories deep,
Horizons where the sunsets glow.

Among the stars and midnight hues,
Ethereal whispers gently speak,
Of dreams that blend with morning's dew,
In timeless troves, answers we seek.

Beyond the veil of waking thought,
Lies a world where wishes roam,
Each dreamscape with wonder is fraught,
In this endless, boundless home.

Crystal streams and golden sands,
Imagination's purest flight,
Crafting lands with unseen hands,
Bringing darkness into light.

Here, dreams are seeds that bloom anew,
In timeless soils rich and deep,
Awake, our hearts shall journey through,
Dreamscapes where our souls can leap.

Suspended Wonders

In silence hangs the universe,
Suspended wonders quietly spin,
Every star, a solemn verse,
In the vastness, we begin.

Galaxies like twinkling shards,
Drawn in cosmic dance on high,
Mysteries held in stardust guards,
Whispering stories to the sky.

Planets pass with silent grace,
Orbits woven in time's thread,
Through the void, their paths interlace,
In a cosmic, tranquil spread.

Nebulas bloom with cosmic fire,
Colors blending in the night,
In this celestial, grand empire,
Suspended wonders burn so bright.

In the stillness of the stars,
Questions rise and answers gleam,
Suspended wonders heal our scars,
Awakening us from the dream.

Dawn of Ideas

At dawn, the mind's horizon glows,
With ideas bright and visions clear,
In whispers soft, the wisdom flows,
From silence into thoughts we steer.

The birth of concepts in the light,
Seeds of knowledge gently sown,
Chasing shadows of the night,
Bringing forth what was unknown.

In beams of hope and glows of gold,
Ideas flourish, bold and free,
In every thought we grasp and hold,
Lies the dawn of what can be.

Kindled flames of inspiration,
Guide us through the morn's embrace,
Crafting dreams with dedication,
In this sacred, waking space.

From twilight's end to day's bright start,
The dawn of ideas begins to rise,
Igniting passion in the heart,
With endless questions and wise replies.

Printed in the USA
CPSIA information can be obtained
at www.ICGtesting.com
LVHW021134030824
787081LV00015B/28

9 789916 862384